KU-313-680

MUSIC WITH EVERYTHING

G McLaan

# MUSIC WITH EVERYTHING

*Margaret Hope-Brown*

FREDERICK WARNE

Published by
FREDERICK WARNE & CO LTD: London
FREDERICK WARNE & CO INC: New York

© Frederick Warne & Co Ltd
London, England
1973

ISBN 0 7232 1722 X

Printed in Great Britain by
William Clowes & Sons Ltd
London, Colchester & Beccles
394.173

*It is futile to offer children music by which they are bored, or which makes them feel inadequate or frustrated, which may set them against music for ever.*

*I prefer to study the conditions of performance and shape my music to them.*

*I want my music to be of use to people, to enhance their lives.*

BENJAMIN BRITTEN

# CONTENTS

# LIST OF PLATES

# FOREWORD

There seems to be general agreement that we want for our children a fuller, richer life. Music helps to develop a finer aesthetic sense; it offers a chance to participate in something active, creative and joyful. The emotional development of the children seems particularly heightened when music has its rightful place in integrated learning.

Indeed, the thematic approach is the most natural and wholly satisfactory. Music is strongly linked with language, with movement, dance and drama, with visual studies, with social studies, with mathematics and science. Because of this 'whole' integrated approach, children become aware of the full stimulation and enjoyment of learning.

The music in school reflects and influences society. Musical activities in the world at large are brought within the children's experiences at school; on the other hand, parents and other interested people are invited into school to share the children's creativity. As this book so effectively demonstrates, music makes a significant contribution to a fuller, richer life.

D. E. PENNINGTON
*Head Teacher,*
*Baddow Hall Junior School.*

# ACKNOWLEDGEMENTS

My grateful thanks are extended to Mr Benjamin Britten for allowing me to quote some of his remarks on music.

I also wish to acknowledge, with gratitude, the teachers who contributed towards the carrying out of classroom activities connected with the musical ideas contained in this book: Mrs L. M. Lee for helping the children to produce the creative writing on 'Wind and Rain' and 'Light', and who worked with me on the 'Napoleonic paintings' activity; Mrs V. Ainscough, who suggested the idea of 'Musical Photoplay' and who carried out the classroom activities connected with this topic; Mr M. L. Britton for the preparatory work and creative writing about 'The Steam Engine'; Mrs M. W. Ellis, who was involved with me in the work on 'Compositions in music and colour' in an out-of-school activity; Mrs D. A. Bradnam for helping the children to produce the class book 'Our Book of Musical Discoveries'; Miss A. J. Ranson for helping the children to produce the class book 'Musical Words and Pictures'; and Mrs. C. Martin who set the scene for the photograph showing infant work.

I should also like to thank Miss D. E. Pennington, Head Teacher of Baddow Hall Junior School, and Miss E. E. Seabrook, Head Teacher of Baddow Hall Infants School, Great Baddow, Essex, for their constant interest and encouragement. Thanks are also extended to Mr Frank Daunton, for much practical help, and to Rachel Stewart for her valuable assistance and advice in the preparation of the manuscript.

*M. Hope-Brown*

\*     \*     \*

The publisher wishes to thank The Clarendon Press, Oxford, for kindly granting permission for the reproduction of 'The Soldiers' from Frances Wilkins' *Speaking and Moving*, Book One; Schott & Co Ltd for consenting to the reproduction of 'The Mocking Bird Song' from Brian Brocklehurst's *The Pentatonic Song Book*, and the diagrams and material concerning care of instruments from the *Studio 49* catalogue; and Evans Brothers Ltd for the use of quotations taken from the *Music Teacher*. Thanks are also extended to Mr Richard Traube for the photographs on plates A, B, C (bottom), D and H; to Geoff Baker for the photograph on plate C (top); and to the Education Department of Essex County Council for allowing these photographs to be included in the book.

# I

# INTRODUCING CREATIVE MUSIC

A group of children were discussing a topic in which they had become interested.

'Let's make up music about it,' said Carol. 'We can have music with everything!'

Along with more traditional activities such as choral singing, instrumental playing, aural training and listening to music, these children had been encouraged to compose their own music, and working creatively with sound was quite natural to them.

It is about this aspect of their musical activities that this book is written. The ideas it contains are based on the teachings of the composer and educationalist Carl Orff, and adjusted to suit the particular circumstances of the children.

**Experimenting with sound**   The children showed great interest in experimenting with sound and enjoyed exploring musical instruments. This was a rewarding activity, especially in the earlier stages, as it enabled children to distinguish between the various properties of the instruments, and helped to develop an awareness of tone colour that could later be applied to music.

A class of six-year-old children which had been exploring the bar instruments (see appendix A) illustrated the following discoveries using crayon and collage:

We found that we only used the first seven letters of the alphabet in music.
We discovered that all the instruments start with the note C.
We also found that the bars come down in small steps.
We discovered that the biggest bar made the lowest sound and the smallest bar made the highest sound.

Their work was made into a class book, which they called 'Our Book of Musical Discoveries'.

Another group of six-year-old children whose musical explorations were illustrated and made into a class book called 'Musical Words and Pictures', had their work linked with reading activities by arranging their 'musical words' alphabetically:

The *alto* xylophone has 13 notes. You can make low bumpy sounds on it.

1

These *bells* make gentle shivery tinkling sounds.
A pair of *cymbals* can make clashing crashing sounds.

Drawing from their own experiences, the children discovered musical words for each letter of the alphabet. There was some difficulty in finding a word beginning with 'y', but a delightful suggestion was made that summed up their feelings about creative music:

If you play *your* own tune or sound it makes you feel satisfied.

Some older children wanted to compare the compass of the bar instruments, and decided to work in groups with each group investigating one of the instruments. Using a piano to determine the pitch of the note produced by the lowest bar, each group proceeded to work out the compass of their instrument. They then came together to compare their findings and record them by means of a graph (see pl. A).

They wrote about their findings as follows:

We notice that:
1   The soprano glockenspiel produces the highest sounds.
2   The alto xylophone and alto metallophone produce the lowest sounds.*
3   The upper notes of the alto glockenspiel, soprano xylophone and soprano metallophone overlap with the lower notes of the soprano glockenspiel.
4   The lower notes of the alto glockenspiel, soprano xylophone and soprano metallophone overlap with the upper notes of the alto xylophone and alto metallophone.
5   The soprano xylophone and soprano metallophone have the same compass.
6   The alto xylophone and alto metallophone have the same compass.
7   The alto glockenspiel has the same compass as the soprano xylophone and soprano metallophone plus additional bars for the notes G and A at the top.

**Sound pictures**   During a lesson on creative experiment, a group of seven-year-old children chose to explore various sound sources. They talked excitedly about the part of their activity that related to the musical instruments:

'We decided to experiment with the musical instruments and try to find out how they made sounds. We started with the cymbals, and found that if we touched them after we had struck them, we felt a tickle. We decided to do the same thing with the chime bars, and they tickled our fingers, too. Gareth said that he thought this tickle was vibrations, and when we looked up ''vibrations'' in our dictionaries, we found that it meant ''to shake or tremble'' and so we decided that this must be right.'

'Kevin said that it reminded him of ''pinging'' a rubber band, and so we got some

* It should be mentioned that the school did not possess the bass xylophone at that time.

rubber bands to see if we could watch vibrations. It worked quite well, and the rubber bands made an interesting sound.'

'I couldn't feel these vibrations on the metallophone, but I did find that the sound stopped when I put my finger on the bar. I think this must be because I stopped the bar vibrating.'

'Yes, and we also found that the xylophone did not vibrate as long as the metallophone. Siobhan tried experimenting with different beaters on the instruments, and we were surprised at the way the sound changed. Although the note was the same, the harder beaters made a louder, harsher sound.'

'Gareth had another good idea and suggested that we could try striking the wooden sound box of the xylophone to see if it made a nice noise.'

'Yes, and I found that it did. I also found that the different lengths and widths of the wood made different sounds.'

'We discovered a lovely noise on the chime bars. We found that if we struck them and then wiggled our thumbs over the hole in the "barrel" part underneath the metal bar, the sound became louder and softer like waves.'

'We liked this sound that we made by plugging and unplugging the barrel part, and decided that we would like to make a "sound picture" about it.'

One of the children then went on to describe how they had made a pattern of the shapes and colours of the sounds they had discovered in order to create this composition :

'We decided to make our "piece" around the "wavy" sound that we found on the chime bars. Three of us struck chime bars and moved our thumbs over the holes to get the sound we wanted, and as the sound began to die away, the other instruments came in one by one. We all tried to "match" our sounds so that the music seemed right. Sometimes we didn't like the way our piece of music was going, and so we changed our sound shape. When we all liked the sound picture that we had made, we decided that our piece of music was finished.'

Experimenting with sound and exploring the musical instruments stimulated the children's imagination and introduced them to the various qualities of the instruments. It proved to be a most enjoyable and useful activity.

# 2

# EXPLORING RHYTHM

**Speech patterns**   Words were used as a starting point for rhythmic improvisations. When working with young children the most natural words to take were the childrens' own names, although this did not fulfil the requirements for a wide vocabulary of rhythms as so many names fitted into the same rhythmic pattern, for example:

The children were delighted, however, to hear the rhythm of their names clapped, and when names such as John or Joan were encountered (giving no rhythm other than a single sound),

more interest was added by using the child's surname as well:

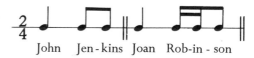

A game which the children called 'guess the name' was introduced. The rhythm of the name of a member of the class was clapped or played on the tambour:

The children had to decide which child was being represented and the first to give the correct answer had a turn in clapping or playing another name. Where several names had the same rhythmic shape, the answer was considered correct if any one of these was given. The children were very interested to hear their names clapped or played on the tambour and lively discussions arose when two or more names with the same rhythm were discovered.

Rhythmic notation was introduced when the children asked to see their 'rhythmic names' written down. This came quite naturally, as the children had experienced the rhythms before the question of writing them down arose. The eventual aim was to encourage the children to relate all their patterns to notation so that when sufficiently experienced, they could record all their improvisations.

For older children the names of football teams, countries, cars, towns and so on held more interest, for example:

These names (or other words chosen for this purpose) were recited against a regular beat which was provided by clapping, foot tapping or keeping a steady pulse on a tambourine or drum.

Interesting contrapuntal rhythms were then performed by dividing the class into groups with each group repeating its own word or words:

The next stage was to ask the children to say the words in their heads and at the same time clap the rhythm of these words in order to become aware of the rhythmic patterns being used.

Further interest was introduced by asking the children to interpret their speech patterns in other sounds, such as a combination of stamping, finger snapping, tapping, clapping and so on:

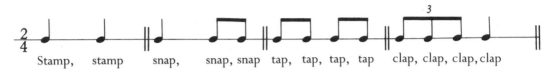

The suggestion was then made that the stamping could be replaced by drums for example, finger snaps by woodblocks, tapping by tambourines, with clapping interpreted on rhythm sticks. The result was an exciting combination of rhythms and tone colours.

In order to perform these rhythms on the various instruments the children had to work in groups. Co-ordination and concentration were developed as each child contributed his own part to the ensemble, and further opportunities for aural training arose through listening for entries and adjusting the balance of sound within the group.

Eventually longer phrases or sentences were used which provided a wider scope for more interesting rhythms:

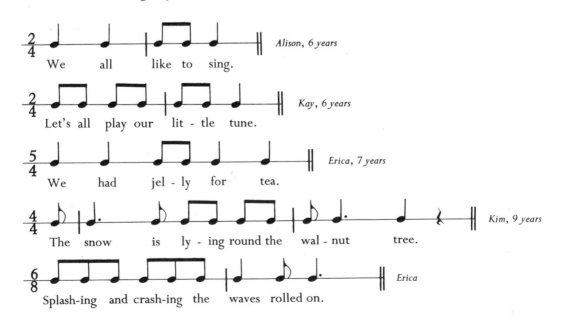

Fresh eggs bu-tter and cream. Come and buy from me. *Sarah, 9 years*

Rags and bones, I am buy-ing rags and bones. *Malcolm, 9 years*

**Developing speech patterns** An interesting development took place while the children were exploring the rhythm of speech, when Carol (aged eight) declared excitedly, 'I have found a poem that we can use for practising rhythm.'

This was quite a major step forward for these children, as until then, their speech exercises had taken the form of short phrases. The poem that Carol had found was 'The Soldiers' from *Speaking and Moving*, Book One, by Frances Wilkins.

### THE SOLDIERS

Speakers: *Soldiers (led by a drummer) and a child.*

SOLDIERS (*marching round the room*):
 Here we come marching,
 Soldiers in red,
 We follow the drummer
 Who drums at the head.

CLASS: Rumpety-tum,
 Rumpety-tum,
 Follow and follow
 And follow the drum.

CHILD (*bowing if a boy, curtsying if a girl*):
 May I come marching,
 Soldiers in red,
 And follow the drummer
 Who drums at the head?

CLASS: Rumpety-tum,
 Rumpety-tum,
 Follow and follow
 And follow the drum.

SOLDIERS: Yes, if you march
 Like soldiers in red,
 And follow the drummer
 Wherever you're led.

CLASS:        Rumpety-tum,
              Rumpety-tum,
              Follow and follow
              And follow the drum.

*(The child marches along behind the soldiers round the room.)* (Repeat)

Carol read the poem aloud for the rest of the class to hear, and the children immediately asked if they could 'try it out'. They discovered that the poem contained a regular pulse which alternated between strong and weak:

Here we come marching,
s               w

Soldiers in red,
s               w

We follow the drummer
  s               w

Who drums at the head.
  s               w

The children decided to indicate these beats by slapping their knees on the strong beats and clapping on the weak beats. They then exchanged ideas on how the poem should be performed. A lively discussion followed, and it was interesting to hear from the tape recorder how the children's ideas developed. The following suggestions were made:

'It would be fun for us all to do the knee slapping right through the poem. It would sound like marching.'

'I think "rumpety-tum" makes a nice sound, it makes me think of drums. Could about four boys keep on saying these words so that it sounds like drums beating?'

'I think that would be a bit difficult. Anyway, "rumpety-tum" is already in the "Class" bit. How about saying it during "Soldiers" and "Child" but having a rest during "Class"?'

'We could start the poem by saying "rumpety-tum" about four times, gradually getting louder so that it sounds like the soldiers coming up the road, and we could end by saying "rumpety-tum" getting softer to sound as though the soldiers are going away again.'

'Let's also say it a couple of times in the middle.'

'The boys with deeper voices should be the soldiers.'

'Could Veronica be "Child"? Her voice is quite high and would make a nice contrast with the boys' voices.'

'Her voice would be drowned by the boys who are saying "rumpety-tum". I think it is a good idea to let girls with high voices say the part, but it would be better to have about six girls instead of one.'

In this way the following performance was devised:

## THE SOLDIERS
*as devised by a class of 8-year-old children*

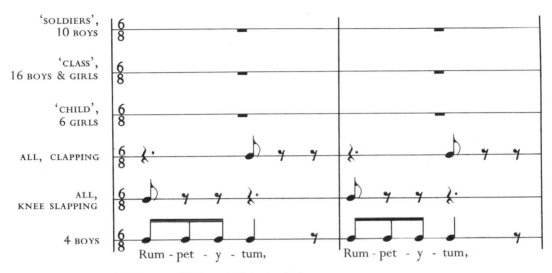

*Starting very softly & gradually getting louder* ------------------------------------------------
(soldiers coming nearer and nearer)

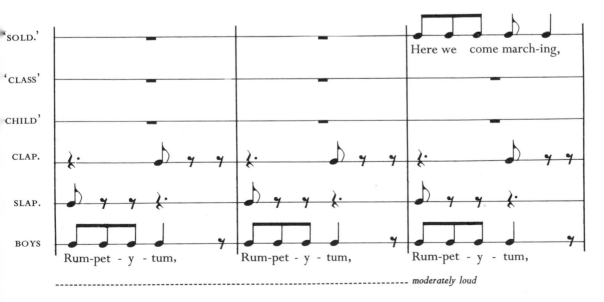

-------------------------------------------------------------------- *moderately loud*

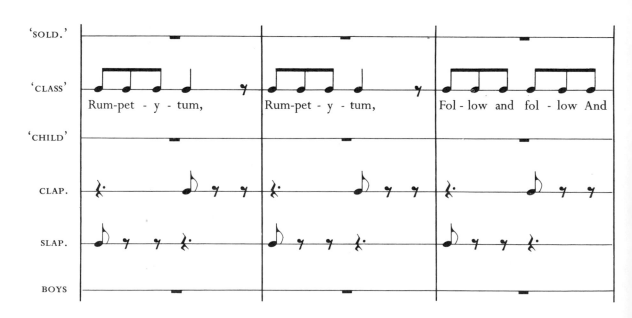

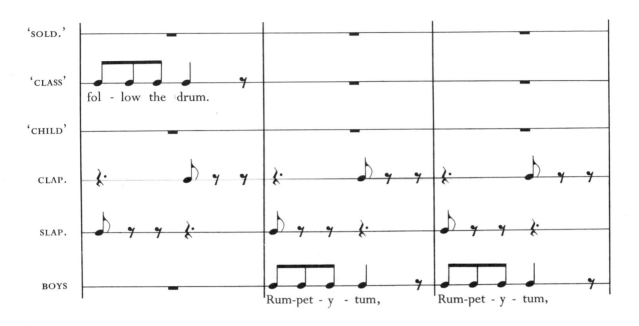

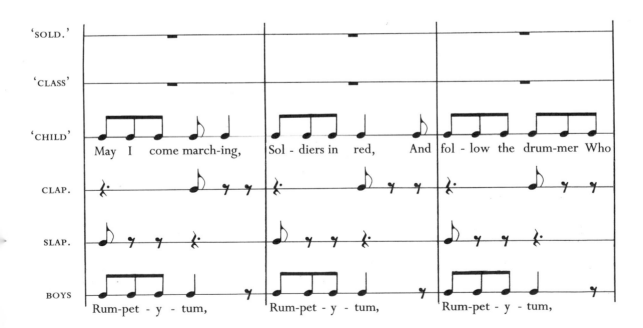

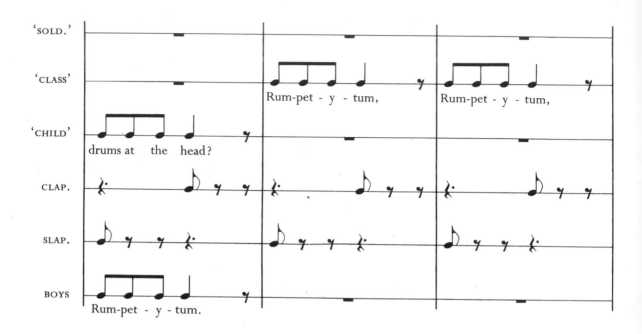

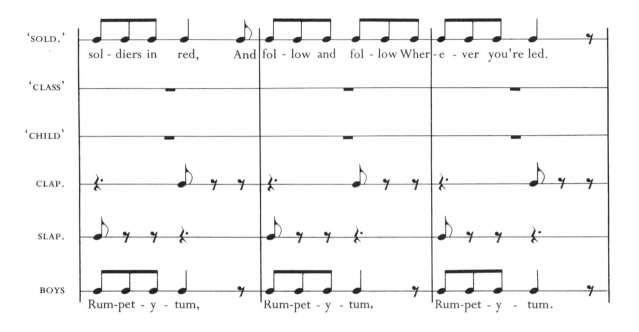

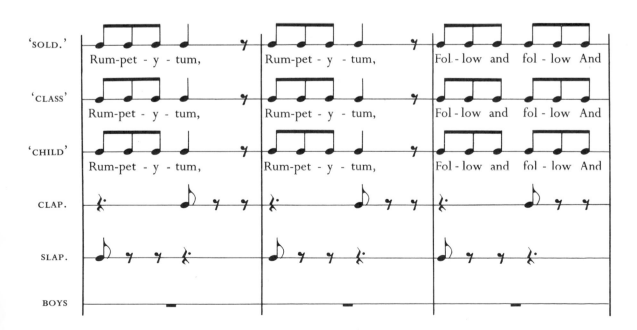

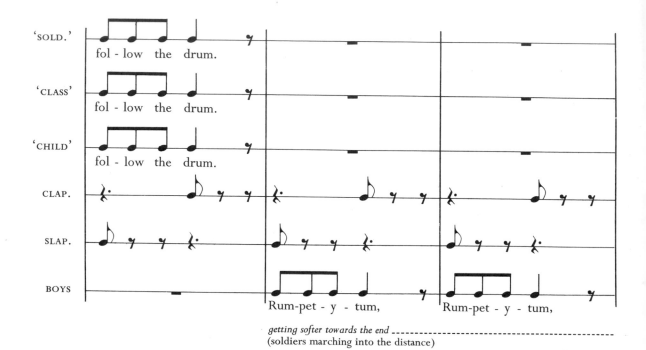

getting softer towards the end -------------------------------------
(soldiers marching into the distance)

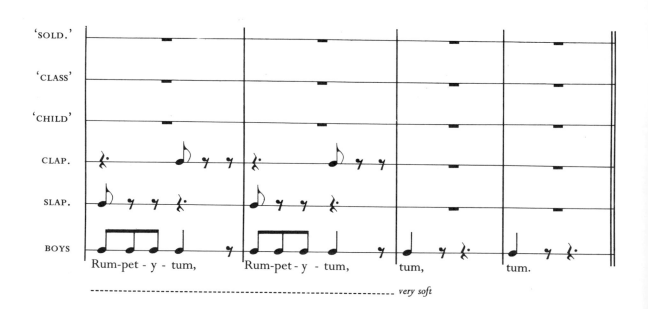

-------------------------------------------------- *very soft*

Many useful teaching points resulted from this work. It was pointed out to the children that they had performed the poem in duple time (two beats in a bar), and this was compared with triple time (three beats in a bar). Note values were brought in when the children asked if they could write down their rhythms. Ensemble work and all that it entails was practised (keeping together, the balance of sound, listening for entries, variations in tone colour, etc.) and, of course, the children were developing their sense of rhythm.

# 3

# DEVELOPING RHYTHM

**Rhythmic imitation**   Rhythms that the children discovered when exploring the metric pattern of speech, were often used as a starting point for rhythmic imitation. The basic idea was that the children imitated a short rhythmic pattern which was clapped to them by the teacher (or another member of the class when the children were more experienced). As soon as the children had repeated this first rhythm, the next pattern was clapped for them to imitate, and so the exercise continued.

It was found that the simplest time with which to begin was duple time:

It was helpful—especially in the early stages—to provide a framework for this activity, in the form of a steady beat. This was either maintained by tapping with the foot, or by letting a reliable member of the class beat quietly on a tambour.

Gradually the degree of difficulty was increased by means of longer phrases,

and other times were introduced, such as triple time,

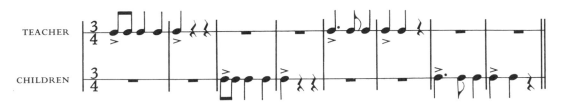

and more complicated rhythms:

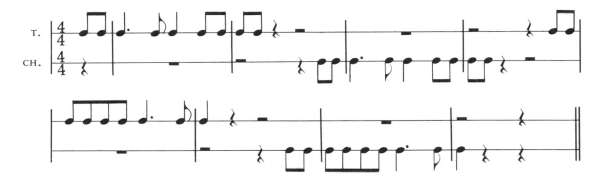

Other activities such as foot stamping, knee and thigh slapping, and finger snapping were gradually included in order to develop a feeling for various tone colours.

A group of eight-year-old children asked if their 'echoing' (as they liked to call it) could be made more difficult by changing the number of beats in the bar each time a new pattern was given to them for imitation. A regular but unaccented beat was established, and in the exercise that followed, continuous changes were made between duple, triple and quadruple times, and phrases that had five or seven beats in the bar were included. This turned out to be a most stimulating activity, and the children thoroughly enjoyed the challenge presented to them by the alternations in time.

These rhythmic exercises of imitative clapping were started simultaneously with the speech exercises described in chapter two, and were used quite extensively. They not only helped to prepare a repertoire of rhythms for the children to use in their improvisations, but also contributed a great deal in developing the children's concentration, memory and aural perception.

**Rhythmic phrase building**  Rhythmic phrase building ('question and answer') developed quite naturally from rhythmic imitation. The clapped patterns that were used previously for the whole class to imitate, became 'questions' to which individual children provided the 'answer'. A short rhythm was clapped as before (see rhythmic imitation), but this time it was directed to an individual member of the class. Instead of the child reproducing the same rhythmic pattern in reply, he provided a complementary rhythm that completed the phrase, thereby giving an 'answer' to the 'question' that had been asked.

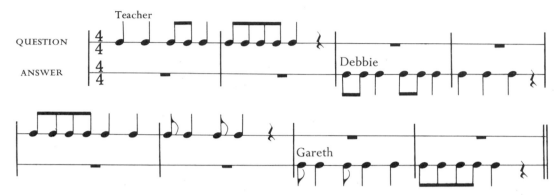

These exercises were carried out either by looking at a child at random, or by going round the class in turn, and every effort was made to avoid breaks in the continuity. It was then suggested that the children could 'talk to each other' with clapped rhythms. This resulted in a lively rhythmic 'conversation' around the class, with the children providing the 'questions' as well as the 'answers'.

As the children became more confident, they added a variety of tone colours by clapping in different ways (using a hollow hand, etc.) and including knee and thigh slapping, foot tapping and finger snapping. Further interest was added by using dynamic changes (loud and soft) and rhythmic accentuation. Eventually individual children were able to create complete phrases, by providing 'answers' to their own 'questions'.

These exercises on completion of rhythms were introduced quite early, in order to develop a sense of form and to lay the foundations for improvisation.

**Rhythmic rondo**    Another development of the previous rhythmic work was the introduction of rhythmic rondo.

It was explained to the children that rondo is a musical form, probably derived from the 'rondeau' which was an early type of song, sometimes accompanied by a dance, in which a solo voice and choral refrain alternated.

A rhythmic phrase that the children had discovered through 'echoing' was used as a starting point for rhythmic rondo. This phrase was established by being clapped for the whole class to imitate.

It was described as the 'chorus' of the rondo, and referred to as the 'A' section. It was explained that this principal theme, or chorus, occurs at least three times in the rondo.* Between each repetition of the principal theme are intervening sections which contain new ideas. These were called 'B' and 'C', and it was suggested that they should be improvised by two soloists. Therefore the rondo form A B A C A was built up. The children then performed the rhythmic rondo, by playing the principal theme A all together, with the intervening sections B and C being improvised by soloists in turn. In the following example a coda was also added to give a greater sense of finality.

* Sometimes a third episode may occur, in which case the principal theme appears four times.

This provided a further exercise in developing a feeling for form, and also gave an opportunity for combining imitation with free improvisation.

The children were very interested to learn that many composers had used this musical form, and the work provided an excellent opportunity for introducing listening music such as Mozart's Pianoforte Rondo in A minor, and the 'Vivace' from Beethoven's Pianoforte Sonata in G major (op. 79). The children were most appreciative of this music, because they associated themselves with it. As Stella (aged nine) said, 'It is exciting to think that we are composing music in the same shape that Mozart and Beethoven used.'

**Rhythmic canon**    The use of imitation in simple canon presented a new challenge to the children. It was explained that in this form, the parts overlap.

The children did not learn the entire rhythmic sentence before performing it in canon (as in learning to sing a 'round'). The canon was performed by imitating each phrase as it was presented, (i.e. rhythmic imitation but with the parts overlapping) and usually made up as the children went along.

The children found this more difficult at first, and the canons were kept very simple. It was suggested that the 'echo' should have a different tone colour, so that it could be easily distinguished, as in the following example. This canon was created by Susan and Mark, both aged nine:

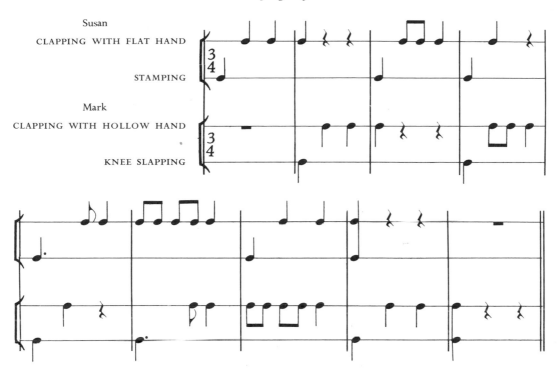

Once the children had grasped the idea of imitation in canon form, it became a favourite activity.

**Rhythmic ostinato** A class of children had already been introduced to the principle of verbal ostinato through the repetition of the 'rumpety-tum' phrase that accompanied 'The Soldiers' (see pages 8–9). In this case the idea of ostinato as accompaniment had arisen spontaneously as a result of the children's reactions to the words of the poem. It was explained that a true ostinato consisted of a phrase repeated over and over again.

Ostinato in its rhythmic form was often developed from a short rhythm pattern which had been discovered through a 'question and answer' exercise, for example:

This phrase was first established by imitation, and then used in continuous repetition:

Thus a rhythmic ostinato was created. One of the children, age six years, was then asked to improvise a rhythm over this ostinato by listening carefully to the 'accompaniment' and creating a rhythmic phrase that 'matched'.

The children were encouraged to listen most carefully to the sounds that they were producing, in order to achieve a good balance between improvisation and 'accompaniment'. If the children were not satisfied with the balance of sound, they held discussions on how it should be improved. Their suggestions ranged from having the ostinato performed by the whole class—but very quietly—to limiting the number of performers according to the effect required.

Through simple ostinato rhythms using stamping as well as clapping,

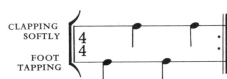

the children gradually progressed to creating ostinato rhythms that were more complex,

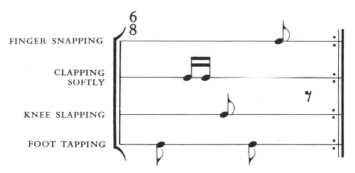

to provide a basis for their improvisations.

The rhythmic ostinato played a very important part in all forms of improvisation.

\*　　\*　　\*

As the children became more confident in their rhythmic work, they began to include more tonal variety. For example, ostinato rhythms were performed on the drum and woodblock

and the rhythmic canon sounded very attractive on the tambour and claves. Improvisations created over the rhythmic ostinato sounded very effective on the tambour, and the addition of these instruments to the rhythmic rondo added extra colour.

Developing rhythm through the exercises described in this chapter proved most successful, and the children thoroughly enjoyed their activities. This account has, however, been consolidated and described under various headings for clarity, which do not imply a scheme of work. When a new exercise was introduced, it was used alongside the earlier exercises, for it was not a case of 'off with the old and on with the new', and the order in which the more complex exercises evolved from word patterns and imitation varied according to the abilities of the children and their ages (which ranged from five to eleven years).

It would also be incorrect to infer that the children became fully proficient in all these exercises before working with pitch, since the two aspects of music making were developed simultaneously.

# 4

# CONCEPT OF MELODY

Melodies and their accompaniments were developed in a similar way to rhythm. The speech patterns, and the 'imitation' and 'question and answer' techniques were all treated melodically, and these melodic exercises were sung and/or played on tuned percussion instruments such as xylophones, glockenspiels and so on. Pitch was introduced gradually, and at each stage the work was reinforced with the creation of melodies based on the given number of notes.

**Introducing pitch**  The following examples show how speech rhythms were set to simple melodies, involving a gradually expanding range of notes. The first two to be used were G and E:

When the children had gained proficiency on these two notes, A was added:

The range was then extended to four notes by adding D,

and eventually the note C was included:

These five notes form the pentatonic scale C D E G A:

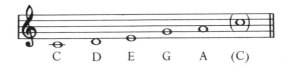

The use of the pentatonic scale for early experiences in improvisation is to be recommended. This scale contains only five different notes (d r m s l), with no interval smaller than a tone. As there are no semitones, the melody can begin and end on any note, and any of the notes in this scale will combine harmonically. This provides a very satisfying basis for the introduction of group improvisation.

    While the work was being consolidated in this pentatonic, tunes were centred around the different notes contained in the scale, for example the note A was used as the tonal centre:

Fresh eggs but-ter and cream, Come and buy from me. *Sarah's tune (9 years)*

This explored the minor flavour of the pentatonic scale, which was then compared with the major effect of a tune centred on C:

Rags and bones! I am buy-ing rags and bones. *Malcolm's tune (9 years)*

When the children became familiar with the pattern and sound of the pentatonic scale, it was pitched on other notes, e.g.:

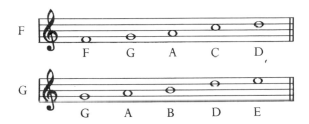

As most diatonic bar instruments are constructed with interchangeable bars for the notes of the scale of C major (together with the bars F sharp and B flat within the compass of the instrument*) the above pentatonic scales were accommodated without any difficulty, and by removing the bar for F and replacing it with the bar for F sharp the pentatonic based on D was available:

Introducing pitch in this way not only provided a sound method of extending the range for melodic improvisations but also supplied an excellent opportunity for bringing in elementary musical notation. As each note was presented the children were shown how to write it down, and eventually learned to associate the sound with

---

* It should be mentioned that the bars for C sharp, D sharp and G sharp are also available, enabling the instruments to be used in all keys. Alternatively a diatonic instrument can be converted to chromatic by obtaining a chromatic resonance box with the extra notes that do not belong to the diatonic instrument.

the symbol. They were then encouraged to write down their improvisations, and their music reading was improved by an interchange of manuscripts between the groups in order to play each other's tunes.

Using the pentatonic range of notes when introducing melody making, gave the children a firm foundation upon which to build. As their musical experiences widened, the range of notes was extended to include modes,

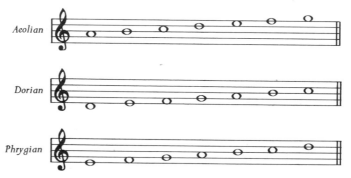

major and minor scales, and more unusual scales including the 'artificial' in which individual children created their own note-rows.

**The drone as accompaniment**   The simple drone (doh and soh sounded together) played on tuned percussion instruments, especially xylophones, was used to accompany melodic exercises. Pentatonic melodies sounded effective with this type of accompaniment, and when the children were using notes from the pentatonic scale pitched on C in their early melodic work, the notes C and G formed the drone.

The lowest note of the drone establishes the tonal centre, so the drone was changed to A and E when the tonality of the melody was centred around A.

The following examples show some of the drones which accompanied the children's melodic exercises:

As they became more experienced, they also began to use easy moving drones:

These provided an ostinato accompaniment (compare with rhythmic ostinato, page 21), and were later developed into melodic ostinati that were more complex, as described on page 35.

**Imitation and phrase building using melody**   The techniques of 'imitation' and 'question and answer' (see chapter three) were used melodically. These exercises were carried out vocally and on tuned percussion instruments, over the support of a drone bass.

The following examples show some of the melodic exercises created by children using the gradually increasing range of notes described in 'Introducing Pitch' on page 25.

Imitation using two notes:

* See footnote on p. 30.

Imitation using three notes:

Question and answer, with four notes:

\* All instrumental parts are written in the lower range of the treble clef for ease of reading. The actual pitch of the music is, of course, one or two octaves higher or lower, depending upon the range of instruments used (see diagram on p. 60).

Question and answer using five notes:

These melodic exercises provided good aural training, and an excellent introduction to improvisation through the simultaneous invention and performance of both rhythm and melody.

An interesting activity took place when introducing vocal improvisation to a class of nine-year-old children. After preparatory work in the form of melodic imitation and melodic phrase building had been carried out using a widening range of notes, it was agreed that there should be no more speaking in the class at all and all the conversation should be sung. The children found this was great fun and were soon vocalizing freely. Obviously the standard varied a great deal, as did the length of the replies that the children gave to the sung questions, but the main object was achieved in that all the children had participated in this form of improvisation at their own speed and level of ability.

An example of a conversation that took place is as follows:

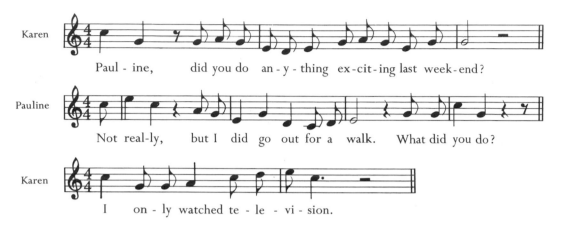

**Melodic rondo**   The melodic rondo was a further development of the rhythmic rondo (see page 18). Its form (A B A C A) provided an opportunity for combining melodic imitation and improvisation.

Three nine-year-old children asked if they could make up a melodic rondo around one of the phrases discovered through melodic 'question and answer'. The theme that they chose for A was performed on an alto xylophone

and accompanied by a drone on the bass xylophone:

They decided that the improvised sections B and C should be played on the soprano xylophone.

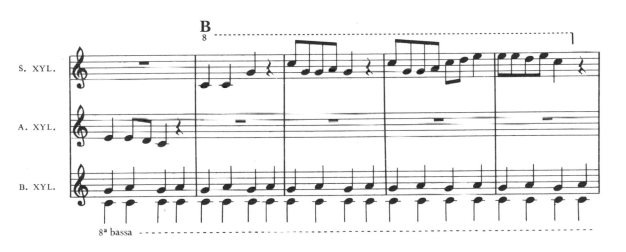

This created a melodic rondo in a very simple form. As the children became more advanced musically, and experienced in group improvisation, their rondos became more complex both in content and texture.

**Melodic canon**   The melodic canon was a development of melodic imitation (page 29) and rhythmic canon (page 20). These canon exercises were performed vocally (as in a 'round') and on tuned percussion instruments. The latter approach usually required a little more skill, and it often proved advisable to restrict the number of notes being used, especially with younger or less musically gifted children.

As with the rhythmic canons, the children did not learn the complete tune before performing it 'in canon'. Each phrase was imitated as it was presented, but with the parts overlapping. The canon exercises were supported by a drone bass (particularly important when being performed vocally) which was usually played on a xylophone.

**The melodic ostinato**   The melodic ostinato, in which a short melodic phrase was repeated over and over again, grew from the drones described on page 28.

One of the reasons for introducing pitch through the pentatonic now became particularly apparent. The harmonically satisfying combination of notes to be found in this scale, together with the repetitive nature of the ostinato, enabled the children to create original melodic accompaniments at an early stage in their musical development. These ostinato accompaniments provided an excellent foundation upon which soloists could improvise.

The children had been introduced to this idea of using a phrase in continual repetition as a basis for improvisation through the rhythmic ostinato (page 21), and the similar use of pentatonic themes presented few problems. When the melodic range was extended to include major and minor scales and modes, the accompaniments were again founded on harmony that grew out of the drone bass, with the later addition of ostinati and chords on other notes of the scale.

Major:

Minor:
(This ostinato was also used in the Dorian mode without the flat.)

Tonic and supertonic triads, major:
(The children did not use this as a 'moving drone'. A definite change of harmony occurred at* forming an interesting accompaniment to the old song 'Sumer is icumen in'.)

Tonic and mediant triads, the melody line being in the Aeolian mode:

*(right)*
Exploring
the instruments

PLATE A

*(below)*
Compasses of
bar instruments
compared

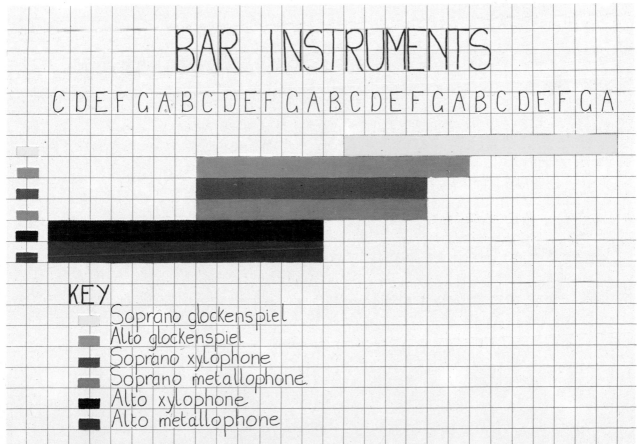

BAR INSTRUMENTS

C D E F G A B C D E F G A B C D E F G A B C D E F G A

KEY

Soprano glockenspiel
Alto glockenspiel
Soprano xylophone
Soprano metallophone
Alto xylophone
Alto metallophone

Discussing
discoveries

*PLATE B*

Developing
melody maki

PLATE C    (*above*) Preparing an ostinato

(*right*)
Improvising
over an ostinato

PLATE D    Creating a tone-poem

*PLATE E*     Rhythm and movement with painting

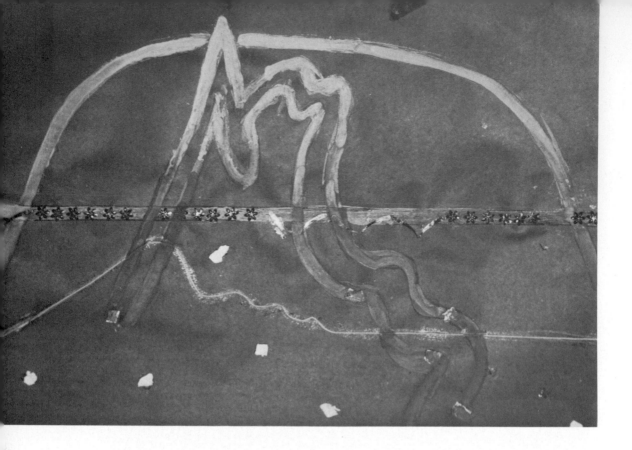

PLATE F     Compositions in music and colour

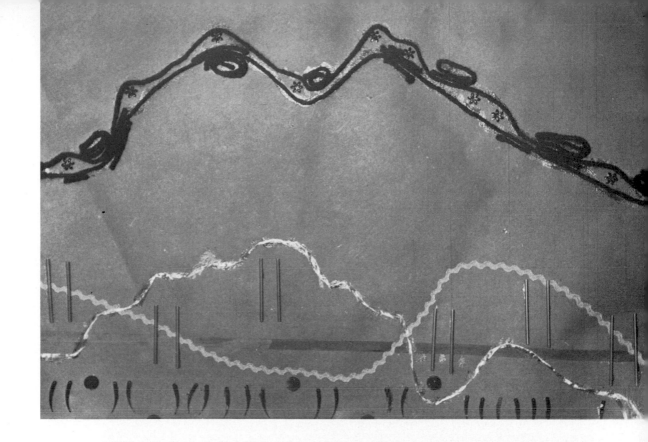

PLATE G
Compositions in music
and colour

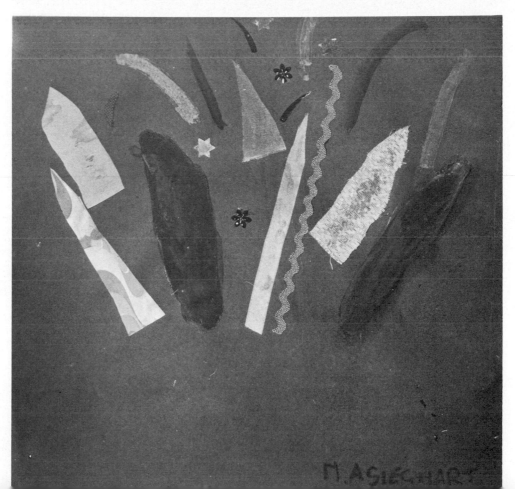

(*above*) *A selection of instruments:* bongo drums, tambourines, tambour, triangles, woodblocks and cymbals

## PLATE H

(*below*) *Tuned percussion instruments:* xylophones, metallophones, and glockenspiels with beaters

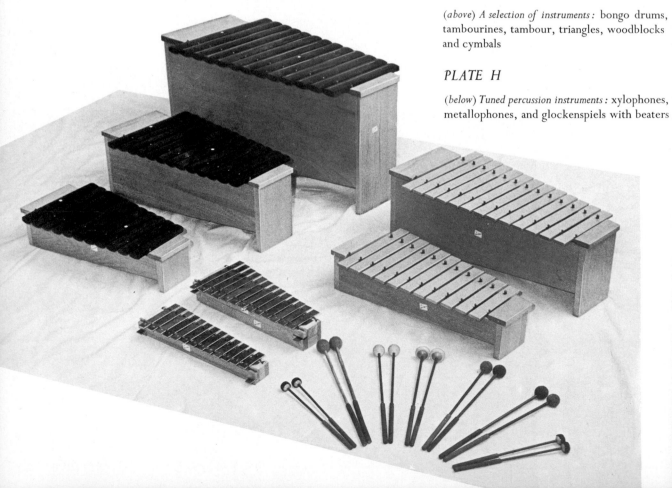

As these ostinato accompaniments became more complex and freer in style, the improvisation of solo melodies required more skill. Great importance was attached to the fact that the soloists needed to capture the characteristics of the accompanying ostinato in their melodic line. Most of the children achieved this through their natural sense of musicianship, and any failure was usually the result of inattentive listening. This was resolved by encouraging the children concerned to listen more carefully to the introductory ostinato being played.

Although the children included other forms of accompaniment in their ensemble playing as they became more experienced, the ostinato always held an important place in the development of musical creativity.

\*       \*       \*

These various approaches to melody making produced very satisfying results which certainly fulfilled a dictionary definition: 'Melody—a musically pleasing succession of notes.'

# 5

# DESCRIPTIVE MUSIC

Using the effects of tone to create 'atmospheric sound pictures' was another form of music making that had great appeal for children of all ages, and they often chose to add this descriptive music to creative writing that had arisen from work on topics in which they had become interested.

**The music of everyday sounds**   A group of children (average age ten years) had been discussing 'wind and rain' and chose this as their theme for creative writing. In order that no child should feel left out, lines were taken from the work of each member of the group and the result was a poem in which all had participated.

> The wind, the wind whistles through the door,
> Trees are swaying briskly.
> Leaves are blown in all directions.
> Apples from the market are rolling with the wind.
> People are putting their collars up.
> Flower heads are beaten from their stems.
> The wind cuts my face.
> It's like sharp icicles piercing my skin.
> A fierce wind, the March wind.
> Dustbin lids are lifted.
> They clatter down the street.
>
> The rubbish is spilt all over the road.
> People's hats are blown off.
> The hats roll down the street.
> A piece of paper is lifted.
> The wind comes galloping over the hills.
> Everything shudders, nothing is still.
> It pulls at the trees and tugs at the grass.
> It comes along wild and furious.
> It whips up waves on the brook
> As it gallops by.

The final result was read to the children who were encouraged to express the poem in musical sounds.

Mouth sounds were used for 'The wind whistles through the door'. 'Apples from the market are rolling with the wind' was described on a xylophone thus producing a 'wooden' sound which, for the child, represented the texture of apples. The glockenspiel was chosen to illustrate the lines 'The wind cuts my face, It is like sharp icicles piercing my skin', and various instruments of indefinite pitch described the metallic sounds of 'Dustbin lids are lifted. They clatter down the street.'

When working on this part of the poem, one boy who chose to describe the sound of dustbin lids found difficulty in expressing himself in the way he wished. At that moment a dustcart arrived outside the hall in which the lesson was being held, and the dustmen began emptying the bins. Nicholas went outside and after listening intently for a while, came back and picked up a tambourine. He then returned to the dustcart and listened to the sounds being made, at the same time experimenting with the tambourine in order to produce the desired effect. With great jubilation he rushed back to rejoin the group, striking and shaking the tambourine with a very good interpretation of the sounds he had heard.

One of the results of this activity was that the children were encouraged to listen to everyday sounds, and discover ways of expressing them in music.

**Atmospheric music**    Another group of ten-year-old children explored the idea of 'light', with particular emphasis on 'starlight' and 'moonlight'. They, too, wished to add descriptive music to creative writing that had arisen from this theme.

> Twinkling in the silent sky
> Stars shed their shimmering, glimmering, glowing radiance.
> Golden light twinkling down on the earth below.
> The stars of heaven appear to lighten the pitch-black sky.
> Silvery shadows everywhere.
> Starlight is welcome,
> How wonderful the light is.
> The moon creeps out to help the stars,
> Then drifting clouds float across the moon.
> All is dark for a brief moment.
> Brilliant was the eastern star
> That moved on, giving precious light
> For three kings to follow.
> A heavenly beam pours over them.
> As morning comes the starlight fades away.

During the preliminary discussion, the 'starlight' sound was created by a child who wanted to describe in music her feelings during an imaginary walk along a quiet country lane under the light of the stars. Two children chose to add to this musical effect by playing light glissandos to establish the atmosphere of starlight. All three children chose the glockenspiel as the instrument that they felt produced the most satisfying sounds.

These children were joined by another group singing a tune which they called their 'theme of light':

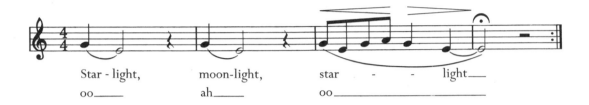

They chose to sing this little melody at various appropriate points during the performance of the poem.

'Golden light' was described on chime bars, and the 'moon sound' beautifully produced on metallophones. In 'The stars of heaven appear to lighten the pitch-black sky', the children playing starlight music were joined by a boy creating a slow crescendo on the cymbal, and the singers sang their theme of light with powerful yet controlled intensity.

In this way a simple but effective tone-poem was gradually created, building towards a climax in the line 'A heavenly beam pours over them'. The poem was read by three children who paused at suitable places for the music to be given full expression, and in the final line, voices, instruments and choral speech all subsided in a gradual and most effective diminuendo.

A very interesting development occurred at the conclusion of this work when the child who played the bass xylophone suddenly took up part of the 'theme of light' and developed it into an ostinato. The other children joined in spontaneously, adapting their themes to capture the characteristics of this ostinato, and a delightful composition emerged.

**Descriptive ostinati**   As part of an exploration into a science project, a class of children, average age nine years, had built a small primitive steam-engine which they described in creative writing:

> The engine is steaming
> The steam is going everywhere
> Out of the funnel, out of the whistle
> Steam here, steam there.
> The whirring steaming thing
> Clatters as the wheel spins.
> Roaring hissing steam streams from the boiler,
> Water comes bubbling from the funnel,
> The piston whizzes round.
> Hot fiery monster
> Spitting water
> Bang clatter
> Steaming noisy engine.
> Smelly hot meths
> Chemist smells.
> Steam spurting out
> Shaking, spitting,
> Water going everywhere.
> Flames leaping up,
> The wheel gradually turns,
> Soon the wheel flies round.

The children decided to say the poem over a verbal ostinato, and the lines chosen were:

> Hot fiery monster
> Spitting water
> Bang clatter.

These three lines were to be repeated continuously by a small group of boys and a small group of girls.

| Boys: | Hot fiery monster | | Bang clatter |
| Girls: | | Spitting water | Bang clatter |

The poem was introduced by a boy slowly hissing 'Steam, steam.' The ostinato then began in a quiet rhythmic manner and was repeated throughout the reading of the poem. The effect was most impressive, the accompaniment giving extra impact to the words of the poem by creating the sensation of a steam engine in motion.

Although this performance was very satisfactory in itself, the children wanted to develop the idea further. The speech rhythms of the ostinato were translated into percussive sounds made first with the hands and feet, and then played on tambour, woodblock and drums:

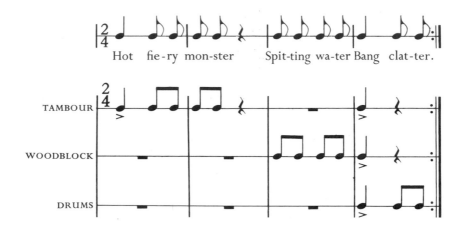

The poem was read again, accompanied this time by the rhythmic ostinato.

The children then wanted to translate these ideas into melody, and took notes of the pentatonic scale pitched on C:

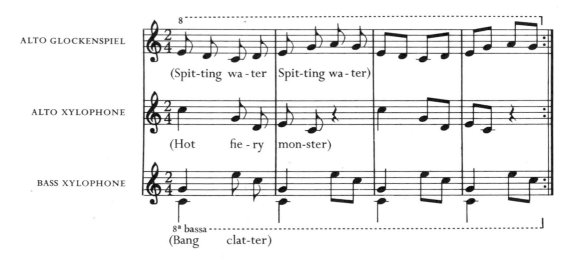

The above accompaniment was then used to provide a background for melodic improvisations (both vocal and instrumental) based on selected lines in the poem.

This account of creativity around the theme of 'the steam engine' enabled the children to discover that ostinato could be used in several forms—verbal, rhythmic and melodic, to enhance the descriptive element of their work.

The children also enjoyed adding descriptive music to some of the poems that they found in their poetry books, and decided to keep a notebook in which to record any suitable verses as they were discovered. Older children kept individual anthologies, whereas descriptive phrases chosen by younger children were illustrated in a colourful way with various media, such as collage, painting and drawing, and made into a class book.

Using music to describe or heighten an idea or situation helped to stimulate the musical initiative of the children, and made them more aware of the effects of tone. The integration of music with language proved particularly successful in introducing this form of creative music making.

# 6

# MUSIC WITH ART

**Rhythm and movement with art**  It was suggested to a class of ten-year-old children that they could improvise percussive phrases for movement sequences and that this could be a group activity, with each group producing its own phrases and choreography. In discussion, the children chose to use interesting speech patterns as a starting point (see chapter two) and decided that the work should be held together by a common theme. At that time the children were working on a topic on the eighteenth century, and had become interested in the Napoleonic wars. It was not surprising, therefore, that this was chosen as their theme.

Words such as 'Napoleonic' and 'cannons booming' were used to provide a basis for rhythmic patterns that were improvised on tambours,

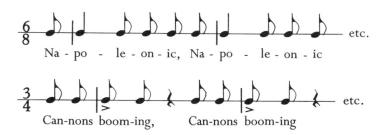

and the children interpreted these rhythms in movement.

It was noticed that patterns of movement were created, giving the free movement shape (for example, moving in circles and along straight and twisted lines) and the idea was put to the children that the shapes made in their movements could be painted on a large sheet of paper, and the character of these movements could be expressed in colour and texture (e.g. light, strong, spiky, thin, wide, etc.). This suggestion was carried out with enthusiasm, and gradually abstract paintings made up of interesting shapes and colours were produced.

Children were then invited to complete the paintings by filling in the spaces and turning the shapes into any object which they felt was represented by the lines. The paintings that were produced had great impact in both feeling for movement and colour (see pl. E).

This idea was linked with further classroom activities when the children wrote about the paintings and described their reactions to them. The creative writing was very varied because the children had individual ideas about what they saw in the painting. This writing was then interpreted musically, both descriptively and melodically, using the approaches described in previous chapters, resulting in further experiences in linking music with language and art.

**Compositions in music and colour**    Further experiments with music and art were made when children painted sounds inspired by music created in a previous lesson. The rise and fall of melody was represented by sweeping lines, and percussive sounds shown as concentrated areas of paint, with the children choosing colours that they felt best described the sounds they heard.

Work with collage was carried out when children expressed a wish to interpret their own creative music in original compositions in colour, using a variety of materials. The ages of these children ranged from four years to sixteen years and they were grouped accordingly. They were invited to improvise freely on the tuned percussion instruments and their ideas were combined to form a musical composition. Melodies which were worked out on the recorder and with voice were accompanied by various ostinati on xylophones and glockenspiels with the addition of tambours, tambourines, cymbals and woodblocks for percussive effects.

On this occasion the children preferred to build up their own collage individually, and described their feelings as they worked.

Loyce (aged 13) wrote of her picture (see pl. F, top):

> The subject of my collage was a piece of music played by several different instruments. One instrument played the same chords again and again and I compared this with the other parts in my picture.
>
> I used the colour yellow to indicate when the music was high, and red to indicate when it was low. I tried to accentuate the actual theme of the music, and placed this theme (which was the same chords the whole time) in the centre.
>
> The rhythmic beating on the woodblock was placed on top of it. One melody seemed to soar, so I represented this with a curved line. The other tune, which was played the whole time in the background, and consisted of two chords played again and again, I placed at the bottom of my picture. I used polystyrene pieces for this in order to represent the actual presence of the tune, without actually interfering with the main part of the music. This picture definitely represented the music to me. I never realized before that sounds could be represented in picture form on paper.

Andrew (aged 12) described his painting as follows (see pl. F, bottom):

> The picture—this is my interpretation of a musical composition made by about eight people. I played the basic ostinato on a xylophone, which went from C to G to E to G over and over again. The lively theme was played on another xylophone, and additional harmony was provided by two glockenspiels and a metallophone, which played a chord. This formed a chorus, after which each instrument improvised upon the chorus in turn.
>
> In the picture, the large, brown zig-zag line is my tune, the red wavy line is the theme and the other prominent lines travelling across the paper are the others' parts in the chorus. The spirals, flourishes, 'explosion' and the 'steps' depict the modifications and improvisations, and the same colours usually mean that one is the improvisation and one the chorus on the same instrument (e.g. the red line across the very top of the picture is the improvisation on the main theme). The background is the atmosphere.

Merril (aged 14) created a melodic line around which some music was developed, by improvising on her recorder. She described her collage as follows (see pl. G, top):

> As I listened to our music, not only did I hear the collective harmonization as it progressed in a solid form, but I was also aware of each individual instrument playing its own melody and following its own course. This is how I decided to record the music in my collage.
>
> The first thing I did was describe the repetitive bass which played the same sequence of notes over and over again. In a regular pattern, and using the materials available to me I represented the bass at the bottom of my composition as this seemed the best place for what was the 'foundation' of my collage.
>
> After this came the intermediary instruments whose individual paths weaved through each other in a very satisfying way. I put these 'melody lines' a little further up the picture, showing the weaving parts of the glockenspiel and xylophone describing their raising and lowering of pitch and their intermingling shown by the overlapping of materials.
>
> Of course my own recorder part held supremacy as far as I was concerned, as my own melody sang out very clearly to me. I put my own part at the top of the collage once again describing alterations in pitch. I also indicated the strong pulse of the melody (the first beat of each bar) with the aid of small plastic star shapes fixed in with my melody line.
>
> Colour was not an important factor to me, although I often hear music in colour. What was most important to me was the shape of everything. Making it look like the music I had heard.

Other children of varying ages and abilities also produced exciting collage to illustrate the same music and a six-year-old boy who had been working independently on the theme of 'fireworks' interpreted his own creative music in collage (see pl. G, bottom).

\*          \*          \*

The above approach provided an excellent opportunity for the introduction of 'listening music'. For instance, when the children learned that Debussy worked with tone as painters did with light, they were anxious to learn more about the Impressionist School, showing great enthusiasm for this music, and several visited art galleries to see Impressionist paintings.

All in all, linking the creativity of music with that of art proved a popular and rewarding activity that provided many of the children with new experiences in both these subjects.

# 7

# MUSICAL PHOTOPLAY

'Photoplay' is essentially the arrangements of projected photographic stills into a sequence, with the addition of sound, to tell a story.

A class of eight-year-old children took part in a project which they called 'The School and its Surroundings'. This involved investigating the area around the school and integrating all possible subjects (nature, mathematics, English, etc.). Each child contributed, and in addition it was decided to film some stills in colour transparencies in order to have a permanent record of the work, and as an experiment which might lead subsequently to more ambitious projects.

The contrast between the old school, which was a few hundred yards away, and the new school (opened three years previously) brought the children into the situation of looking more closely at what they had to enjoy—their new school.

Lively discussions took place on how to get this across on film and the best shots to take. The children decided on a list of stills, but then the question of sound arose. It was pointed out that this was a very important aspect of the project, as sound would strengthen continuity, help the children to recall past events and add greatly to the enjoyment. If the children could provide the sound themselves, they would have a great sense of personal achievement and the joy of taking part.

It was decided that the simplest type of sound track was commentary, and this presented no problem, as the children were used to giving their own comments and information in discussions. It was then suggested that music would increase the impact, (it is both emotional and aesthetic) and could be used to introduce the slides and provide 'fading out' effects.

This idea was greeted with great enthusiasm, and further discussions took place on how to produce the creative music envisaged in this project. It was decided to use a battery-operated portable tape recorder so that the children could listen to their work and judge it critically, re-recording if necessary.

Three of the slides that provided ideas for creative music were entitled 'Outside the School Gates', 'In the Classroom' and 'On the Riverbank'.

**'Outside the School Gates'**    This was to be the first slide in the series. It was taken one morning just outside the school, showing the gates with the name of the school on them, and children passing through.

In discussion it was decided to create a feeling of 'happy urgency', using the name of the school as a basis for improvisation.

The atmosphere was set by Jocelyn, who began by singing:

Bad-dow Hall    School,        Bad-dow Hall    School

Stella then took up the rhythm of the words, beating this pattern on the side of the xylophone:

She then transferred this rhythm to the alto xylophone and composed an accompaniment in the form of an ostinato,

over which Jocelyn (joined by other children) sang her little tune. The music was turned into ternary form (A B A) when Fiona improvised an instrumental section before Jocelyn's tune was repeated.

etc.

At this point, the class wanted to create an atmosphere of noise and bustle as the children played in the playground, reaching a climax with the ringing of the school bell. Word patterns were chosen as the most suitable vehicle for this section, and in order to stimulate ideas that could be built up to a climax, it was suggested that the children imagined their thoughts and feelings when they were late for school. Neil chose to begin by repeating in an urgent manner:

Hur-ry, hur-ry, hur-ry, hur-ry, School will soon be - gin.

Other children then provided a bustling background by joining in with 'Hurry, hurry' in free rhythm. These word patterns were gradually brought to a climax by getting louder and faster, culminating in the ringing of a bell, at which point all sound dramatically ceased.

When the tape recording was played back to the children, they liked the overall effect but wanted to improve various points of tone colour and ensemble, and the work was re-recorded twice more before the children were satisfied with the result.

**'In the Classroom'**   This slide showed the children busily engaged in group activities. The overall feeling was that of 'being busy' and the children wanted to convey this in their music.

The background was created by a boy describing the activity of painting. He interpreted the movements made by a paint brush as gentle, sweeping glissandos on the metallophone (sliding the beater up and down) with occasional accented notes to represent drops of paint.

Grahame composed a 'busy tune' on the xylophone, and the other children expressed a wish to set words to it so that it could be sung. This presented difficulties as the tune was a little too high for the children's voices, so Grahame transposed it to the pentatonic pitched on G. Words were composed by the children, and Grahame's tune was used as the main theme for the music connected with this slide:

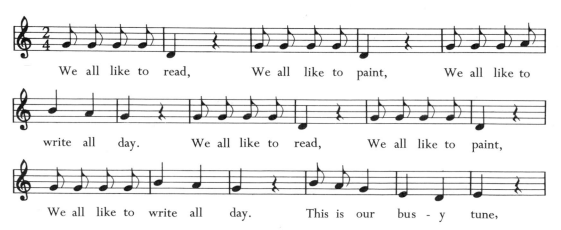

We all like to read, We all like to paint, We all like to write all day. We all like to read, We all like to paint, We all like to write all day. This is our bus-y tune,

This is our bus - y tune. We all like to read,

We all like to paint, We all like to write all day.

Accompaniments in the form of ostinati were worked out on the bass xylophone, and the children sang their song with great enthusiasm. A 'fading out' effect was suggested, implying that the work did not come to a sudden end, but continued day to day. This was achieved by becoming softer and slower towards the end of the tune, with the bass xylophone providing a coda (tailpiece) which faded gradually to silence.

The children were pleased when the recording was played back to them, and it only required one re-recording to achieve a result that they found satisfactory.

After the lesson Grahame was asked about his feelings as he composed his tune. He said, 'First of all I decided on an activity to base my music on. I chose reading because I thought about some of the exciting books I had read. I did not want the large metallophone as the notes lasted for too long. The bass xylophone notes were too low, and the glockenspiel notes were too high, and so I chose the soprano xylophone.

'I chose a group of notes and then I played them over and over again until I had composed my ''busy tune''. Fiona and Stella kept up a steady beat on the bass xylophone which I thought blended very well with my tune.

'I feel very pleased to think that I can compose my own music.'


**'On the Riverbank'** This slide was taken during an educational visit, and was chosen as being particularly suitable for creative music in a descriptive form.

The scene was set by Jocelyn, who described what she was imagining:

'On one side of the bridge the water is flowing very slowly. Under the bridge it is a bit narrower and there it goes faster. Then the water goes to the waterfalls and flows very fast. I will compose music for the slow part, and I will sing it slowly.'

Jocelyn then improvised vocally, composing both words and music as she went along:

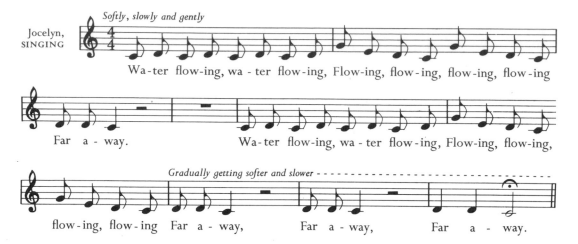

In order to describe the movement of the river while Jocelyn was singing, three children chose to play 'flowing music', using the bass and alto xylophones and the alto metallophone, by sliding the beaters gently but quickly up and down the adjacent bars of the instruments in the form of glissandos. This sounded very effective, but when the recording was played back to the children, they thought it was too 'heavy'. This problem was overcome by transferring the bass xylophone part to the alto xylophone, the alto xylophone part to the soprano xylophone, and the alto metallophone part to the soprano metallophone. The music was re-recorded and the children declared that the balance of sound was 'just right'.

*       *       *

Each of the three examples given in this chapter, shows a different approach to creative music. The first ('Outside the School Gates') is developed through speech patterns, the second ('In the Classroom') shows creativity through melodic improvisations, and the third ('On the Riverbank') is an example of creative music in a freer descriptive form.

'Photoplay' should not be regarded in isolation from the rest of the curriculum as it can be truly integrated into the normal routine of the school. Colourful slides hold the children's attention and at the same time provide material for conversation and creativity, helping to overcome inhibitions.

This form of project is truly audio-visual, and children are proud of work that they have helped to produce. There are very many opportunities for extending and developing musical photoplay.

# 8

# DISCOVERIES THROUGH
# PERFORMANCE

The two aspects of musical creativity—the making of original patterns in sound through improvisation, and the re-creation of established music through performance, were often linked during the lessons, sometimes incorporating 'listening music' as well.

A class of ten-year-old children were singing 'The Mocking Bird Song':

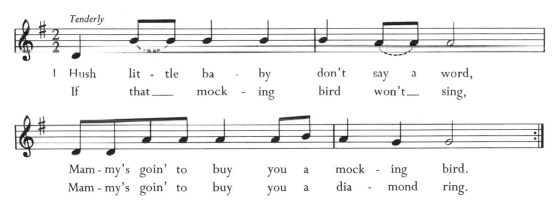

2. If that diamond ring turns brass,
   Mammy's goin' to buy you a looking glass.
   If that looking glass gets broke,
   Mammy's goin' to buy you a billy goat.

As the song progressed, Michael spontaneously clapped a syncopated rhythmic accompaniment:

Gradually all the children joined in with this accompaniment while singing.

The children then chose to develop this idea further by transferring the rhythm to tuned percussion instruments in order to provide their own melodic accompaniment.

As the folk song is one of many that are based on the pentatonic scale (d r m s l d) any of the notes could be effectively combined with no harmonic problems. The only initial decision to be made was in the choice of a pentatonic scale, and the children soon decided that they would use the notes G A B D E.

While providing this accompaniment, an episode was produced between verses resulting in a composition in ternary form (A B A), the A sections being the given tune and the B section an improvisation.

This discovery encouraged another group of children to explore the songs that they had learned in order to find out how many were written in ternary form and they compiled a list with suitable musical quotations.

Listening music in this musical form was then introduced, such as 'Musette in D Major' from *The Anna Magdalena Notebook* by J. S. Bach. One of the children chose to learn to play this piece on the piano and performed it in front of the class during a subsequent lesson.

The children wanted to learn more about Bach and his music and showed a special liking for 'Jesu, Joy of Man's Desiring' when it was played for them on the piano. When it was explained that this piece of music is a chorale in its original form, the children were most enthusiastic in their request to hear the record and were very excited when it was added to the school's record collection. 'Jesu, Joy' (as the children affectionately called it) became a firm favourite and it was not long before the question was asked, 'Can we learn to sing it?'

A simple arrangement was made for voices in unison and the flowing triplets of the first violins and oboe were played with great charm on solo recorder. The problem of playing the long phrases was solved by sharing this part between two players who became so proficient at taking over from each other that it was impossible to tell where the changes took place. The singing of the chorale was incredibly beautiful as the children became completely involved in the music.

Other interesting work evolved from the improvisation of an accompaniment to 'The Mocking Bird Song', which served as a reminder of a further musical form and more 'listening music'. When the children learned the third verse,

> 3. If that billy goat won't pull,
>    Mammy's goin' to buy you a cart and bull.
>    If that cart and bull turn over,
>    Mammy's goin' to buy you a dog named Rover.

and added a second episode to be used between verses, it was pointed out that they were performing in rondo form (A B A C A). The children were very interested to learn how the rondo form had developed, and this led to the introduction of the music of Mozart. Stories of his boyhood fascinated the children and they enjoyed listening to some of his music both on records and performed on the piano. Many asked if they could learn to play some of his pieces on their recorders and arrangements of 'Ah, vous dirai-je maman', 'Ariette' and two of his 'Minuets' taken from *The Beginner Flautist* were learned with enthusiasm and pleasure.

Some of the class decided to prepare written projects on Bach and Mozart, involving them in further research, most of which they chose to do in their own time.

Linking creative and re-creative music proved interesting and stimulating to the children, allowing scope for many of the musical activities that contribute towards a well-balanced musical education.

# 9

# MUSIC AT HOME

The enthusiasm with which children have participated in musical activities at school has often been carried over into the home. Parents have helped in many ways, ranging from keen interest and encouragement to actually sharing the child's new musical experiences, by joining in with the music making at home.

One family decided to form their own little recorder group, with descant and treble recorders for the children, and tenor recorders for mother and father. With the aid of easily understood tutors such as *The New Recorder Tutor* by Stephen Good-year, the learning experience was shared. Music making at home became great fun and was soon the highlight of family entertainment.

Another interesting and useful home activity has been the making of simple instruments. Older children have found great satisfaction in making instruments such as whistles, rubber drums and simple xylophones. The book *Musical Instruments Made to be Played* by Ronald Roberts (Dryad) has provided many ideas.

In the case of younger children, unsophisticated instruments such as shakers have been made at home by taking a cardboard tube of suitable length and cutting two discs of thick card to fit the ends. One end was placed in position using adhesive tape and some rice, sand or buttons etc. were put in the shaker. The open end was covered with one hand and the sound was tested (this helped to develop a discerning ear) and when the child was satisfied with the sound produced, the other end was sealed. The shakers were then decorated and the child experimented with different ways of shaking the instrument in order to discover the most attractive sound. (A see-saw movement was found to be particularly satisfying). Simpler shakers have also been made by placing rice, dried peas and so on into plastic bottles such as those that contained washing-up liquid and these, too, were decorated. The children learned a great deal from making these instruments and discovering how the various sounds were made.

An example of good parental co-operation is to be found in the story of Margaret, who was introduced to music at the age of eight, when she opted to play a woodblock in creative music based on the poem 'The Pied Piper of Hamelin' by Robert Browning, and she soon became an enthusiastic participant in all the school's musical activities.

She particularly loved playing her recorder, and decided that she wanted to learn other instruments as well. Her parents immediately arranged violin lessons for her and these were soon followed by lessons on the piano and oboe.

When discussing her love of music during a lesson at school, Margaret said, 'When I first came to school I could not play any instruments nor read music. The first thing I ever played was a woodblock, and then I was taught to play the tuned percussion instruments. I began to love making music and listening to music, and this soon became my favourite lesson. When I started playing the recorder as well, I found I enjoyed it so much that I wanted to play the violin. Soon I took up the piano and oboe, and I now hope to make music my career.'

Margaret's parents were delighted to discover her growing interest in music. They introduced her to the library in order to find out more about music and musicians, and took her to concerts whenever possible. They gave continual encouragement, liaising with the school for advice, complementing school music with music at home, and attending all school concerts.

Another example was given by Alison (aged ten years) who described the way in which her family had been affected by her love of music. 'I had not been very interested in music before I started to learn it at school. My first instrument was a xylophone, and as my love of music grew, I became interested in learning the recorder. I played every night when I got home, and soon I began to long to play another instrument as well, and I chose the violin. After a while, all my sisters (including my little three-year-old sister) started to like music because I played so much at home.

'I also began learning to play the piano, and soon everyone else in the family began to play, including Mummy and Daddy. All day long someone is playing an instrument at home and there are music books in every room. Even Nana (grandmother) has started to like music and now plays the piano while I play the violin.'

Discussions amongst a group of nine- and ten-year-old children who had been introduced to music through school, disclosed that parental support had enabled several of them to develop their musical interests by means of private lessons. The range of instruments being learned was quite wide, from strings and woodwind to piano and mandoline.

These children were encouraged to play their instruments at school so that other children could have the opportunity of hearing and seeing the instruments that they had heard on records and seen in books. The results were both stimulating and interesting, enabling all the children to share in a wider range of musical experiences. There was an increased interest in orchestral music, because the children found it quite exciting to listen for the instruments that their friends could play. This developed into a love of the music itself, and an increasing awareness of tone colour and orchestral textures. Parents had, therefore, enriched the lives of many other children as well as their own by encouraging music making at home. As one parent joyfully exclaimed, 'A musical renascence has begun in the area.'

# APPENDIX
# A
# THE INSTRUMENTS

The following list includes many of the principal instruments that can be used in creative music.

BAR INSTRUMENTS

**General**  These can be diatonic or chromatic. Diatonic (single row) bar instruments are equipped with interchangeable bars for the notes of the scale of C major, together with the bars F sharp and B flat that lie within the compass of the instrument. Thus the keys of G and F major can be used. The bars for C sharp, D sharp and G sharp are also available, so that if required, the instruments can be used in all keys. With chromatic (two rows) bar instruments, the bars are arranged in piano keyboard order. The lower row corresponds to the white, and the upper row to the black keys. In order to suit the requirements of elementary music making, the bars are interchangeable, as is the case with diatonic bar instruments.

By the addition of an extra chromatic resonance box with the extra notes that do not belong to the diatonic bar instrument, it is possible to convert a diatonic bar instrument into a chromatic one.

*Arrangement of bars*

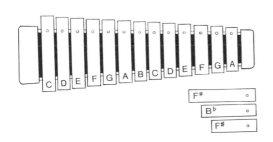

*Diatonic (one row) arrangement of bars*

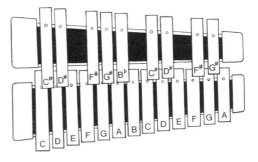

*Chromatic (double row) arrangement of bars*

**Glockenspiels**  Bars made of nickel-plated steel. Models available: Soprano (diatonic and chromatic), Alto (diatonic and chromatic), Alto-soprano (chromatic).

**Xylophones**  Bars made of wood. Models available: Soprano (diatonic and chromatic), Alto (diatonic and chromatic), Alto-soprano (chromatic), Bass (diatonic and chromatic).

**Metallophones**  Bars made of aluminium alloy. Models available: Soprano (diatonic and chromatic), Alto (diatonic and chromatic), Alto-soprano (chromatic), Bass (diatonic and chromatic).

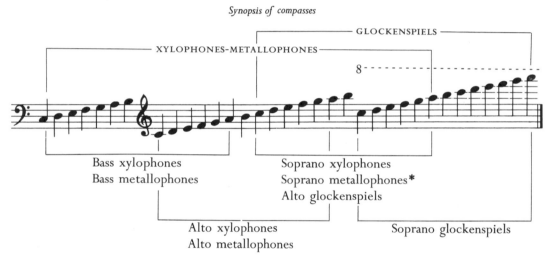

*Synopsis of compasses*

* Some models end on F.

TIMPANI AND VARIOUS DRUMS

**Timpani**  Tunable. Compass about a fifth.

**Other drums**  Bass drum, bongos (stand available), hand drum with double skin, side (snare) drum (adjustable legs or stand available), tambour (hand drum with one skin), tambourine (same as tambour but with jingles).

SMALL PERCUSSION INSTRUMENTS

**Bells**  Bell sticks (small stick with bell on each end), bell spray (different sized bells on leather strap with wooden handle), sleigh bell spray (sleigh bells on leather strap with wooden handle), sleigh bell wristlets (sleigh bells on a lined leather band, either with elastic or with thong for tying).

**Castanets**    Spanish style, with handle (simple or double).

**Claves**    Wooden clicker sticks.

**Cymbals**    Cymbals used in pairs (various sizes), finger cymbals (for wearing on forefinger and thumb), hanging cymbals (various sizes, with hand straps), suspended cymbals (with stand).

**Rattles** (shakers)    Box rattle, cane rattle, gourd, jingles rattle, maracas.

**Resi-resi**    A piece of wood with notches cut across it (often bamboo). Scraped to produce sound.

**Triangles**    Available in several sizes.

**Woodblocks**    With one slit or with two slits (two different notes), tubular (double note).

OTHER MELODIC INSTRUMENTS

**General**    Autoharp, dulcimer, harmonica, melodica. (Drones played on the guitar or 'cello are effective, and a beautiful sound was produced when an eight-year-old boy improvised on the flute, accompanied by xylophones.)

**Chime bars**    Can be purchased separately or in complete sets. Chime bars can be used in small groups, or arranged in both diatonic and chromatic scales.

**Recorders**    Special mention must be made of these, which blend particularly well with tuned percussion instruments and play a vital part in creative music. Descant recorder probably used the most, but other members of the recorder family also used.

# APPENDIX
# B
# CARE OF INSTRUMENTS

**General**  The instruments do not need any special maintenance. It nevertheless seems sensible to draw attention to some important points. Air which is too dry damages the resonance boxes of the bar instruments and after long exposure it can affect the tuning of the xylophones (please use moisturisers in centrally heated rooms!). High temperatures are to be avoided. Wooden instruments and all kinds of drums should not be exposed to radiators or to direct sunlight. Damage is caused by extreme changes of temperature. Condensation will take place when instruments are brought from extremely cold rooms into heated rooms, and this should be avoided.

**Bar instruments**  When removing or interchanging the bars see that they are raised at both ends simultaneously. When bars are 'yanked' off, the pins get bent. Should this happen in spite of careful handling, the pins must be bent back into the correct position very carefully.

**Hand drums**  A common error in tuning hand drums is made by tightening the head unevenly, which causes the wooden shell (rim) to warp after a time and also impairs the best tonal quality of the drum. To tighten, turn thumbscrews not more than $\frac{1}{2}$ turn clockwise, turning each one the same amount, and alternating in this order:

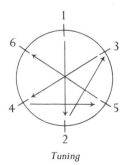

*Tuning*

On hand drums and tambourines having an odd number of tuning screws, alternate as closely as possible to this pattern. If a higher pitch is still desired, start the pattern again with a shorter turn on each thumbscrew.

When finished playing, loosen the head in the same manner, turning counter-clockwise. Be sure to loosen the heads whenever they are not being used, and especially when not in use over an extended period of time.

**All drums**    It is advisable to vaseline or to oil the screws from time to time to ease the tightening and tuning of the instruments and to protect the threads of the screws. A very small drop of oil on the threads occasionally will keep them from corroding and make tuning easier and more accurate. In principle, drums of all kinds should be slackened after use in order to preserve the elasticity of the skin. More serious damage, such as a twisted frame, can happen when a tightly stretched tambour or tambourine is stored for a long time in a dry, overheated room, or if it has not been slackened before the beginning of the heating period. A stretched skin is very suscep-tible to mechanical damage. When storing any drum etc. do be sure that the skin is not in contact with anything sharp, especially not with the screws of tambours or tam-bourines. It is advisable to store hand drums skin to skin, or, if they are the same size, screw to screw. Tambours can also be stored one inside the other. Should a skin get a tear through careless handling, a new skin can be obtained.

*Air-moisture:* It would be a wise precaution, particularly for those who are near the sea, to wipe over the nickel-plated metal parts, including bars of glockenspiels, with a slightly oily rag, because after long usage or storage they are subject to corrosion. This will help to keep rust formation at bay. If rust is already there do not use emery or other abrasives, but clean first with good metal polish suitable for nickel and then apply the slightly oily rag. Metallophone bars are made of an aluminium alloy and cannot rust.

### Suggestions for Classroom Organization

When instruments are kept in a cupboard, it is helpful to label the shelves so that the instruments can be returned to their proper places after use. This enables them to be found easily when needed, and can save time.

In order to avoid beaters being lost or broken, they can either be kept with the appropriate instruments, or stored in a box. The instruments (and beaters) should be easily accessible and well cared for. Enthusiasm and creativity can wane if a required instrument cannot be found, or is damaged.

If chime bars are kept in individual boxes, it is helpful to label both box and lid clearly with the letter name of the chime bar it contains. At the end of each lesson, make sure that each chime bar is returned to its own box along with its beater.

Supplementary bars for the bar instruments should either be kept with the instruments for which they are intended, or placed carefully in a box.

Always keep the instruments free of dust and dirt.

Time spent in training the children to be good 'helpers' is time well spent. Children enjoy the responsibility of looking after the instruments and it encourages them to treat the instruments with respect.

# APPENDIX

# C

# BIBLIOGRAPHY

The following books and music have been found useful when working with children. They represent only a selection of those available, but will serve to provide an introduction.

## Books for classroom use

*Children Make Music* (teacher's book); *Begin Making Music, Make Music, Make More Music* (children's books), Richard ADDISON (Holmes McDougall Ltd.).

*An Introduction to Words and Music* (teacher's guide), *Words and Music* Stages One, Two, Three and Four (children's books), Ian LAWRENCE and Pamela MONTGOMERY (Longman).

*Music in Action* (teacher's guide); *The Sound of the Sea* (Book 1), *The Sound of the City* (Book 2), *The Sound of the Countryside* (Book 3) (children's books), William BULMAN (Rupert Hart-Davis).

*Music Together* (teacher's booklet); *Green Book* (Book 1), *Orange Book* (Book 2), *Blue Book* (Book 3) (children's books), Geoffrey WINTERS (Longman).

*Oxford Instrumental Series* (notes for teachers); *A Christmas Story* (Book 1), *The Boat Race* (Book 2), *Johnny and the Mohawks* (Book 3), *The Frog Princess* (Book 4), *Accompaniments for Selected Songs* (Book 5), *The Magic Fruit* (Book 6), *Drake's Voyage* (Book 7), *The Nightingale* (Book 8), *Accompaniments for Selected Songs* (Book 9) (children's books), edited by Geoffrey WINTERS and Gordon REYNOLDS (Oxford University Press).

## Music

*Eight English Nursery Songs*, Margaret MURRAY (Schott).

*Eighteen Pieces for Descant Recorder and Orff-Instruments*, Margaret MURRAY (Schott).

*Four Christmas Carols*, Margaret MURRAY (Schott).

*Music for Children*, Vol. 1 Pentatonic, Vol. 2 Major: Drone Bass—Triads, Vol. 3 Major: Dominant and Subdominant Triads, Vol. 4 Minor: Drone Bass—Triads, Vol. 5 Minor: Dominant and Subdominant Triads, Carl ORFF, Gunild KEETMAN and Margaret MURRAY (Schott).

*Nursery Rhymes and Songs*, Doreen HALL (Schott).

*Pentatonic Song Book*, Brian BROCKLEHURST (Schott).

*Singing Games and Songs*, Doreen HALL (Schott).

*Songs for Schools*, Keith BISSELL (Schott).
*Timothy's Miracle*, Gwyn ARCH and William MURPHY (Schott).
*Wee Willie Winkie*, Margaret MURRAY (Schott).

## Books for further reading

*Creative Singing*, Ken EVANS (Oxford University Press).
*Elementaria*, Gunild KEETMAN, trans. Margaret Murray (Schott).
*Growing up with Music*, Mary PAPE (Oxford University Press).
*Making Musical Instruments*, Set 2 of 'Lively Craft Cards', Peter H. M. WILLIAMS (Mills & Boon).
*Music for Children* (teacher's manual), Doreen HALL (Schott).
*Musical Instruments in the Classroom*, Geoffrey WINTERS (Longman).
*Orchestral Percussion Technique*, James BLADES (Oxford University Press).
*The Recorder in School*, Freda DINN (Schott).
*Recorder Technique*, A. ROWLAND-JONES (Oxford University Press).

Gramophone records of practical examples from *Music for Children* Volumes 1 and 2 by Carl Orff, Gunild Keetman and Margaret Murray are available (Schott and Co. Ltd.). Both records are introduced and fully explained in the 'Introductory Note and Libretto'.

A great deal of valuable information is also to be found in the Pupils Pamphlets and Notes For The Teacher issued by B.B.C. Publications in connection with the B.B.C. broadcasts to schools (music programmes).

# APPENDIX
# D
# SUITABLE POETRY FOR CREATIVE MUSIC

It would not be possible to list all the books of poetry that can be used for creative music, but the following suggestions are given, as they have been found from personal experience to contain suitable material. Not all the poetry in these books is suitable, and selections should be made. It should be remembered that this short list is by no means comprehensive, and is only offered as a guide.

*All Day Long*, compiled by Pamela WHITLOCK (Oxford University Press).
*The Children's Bells*, Eleanor FARJEON (Oxford University Press).
*Mood and Rhythm* (4 books), chosen by Esme MEARS (A. and C. Black).
*A Puffin Book of Verse*, compiled by Eleanor GRAHAM (Penguin Books).
*Rhyme and Rhythm* (4 books), compiled by GIBSON and WILSON (Macmillan).
*Rhythm and Rhymes*, Ruth SANSOM (A. and C. Black).
*Round the Day*, *Round the Year*, *The World Around*, chosen and arranged by Rumer GODDEN (Macmillan).
*Silly Verse for Kids*, Spike MILLIGAN (Penguin Books).
*Silver, Sand and Snow*, Eleanor FARJEON (Michael Joseph).